It's fun to draw
Princesses
and
Ballerinas

Mark Bergin

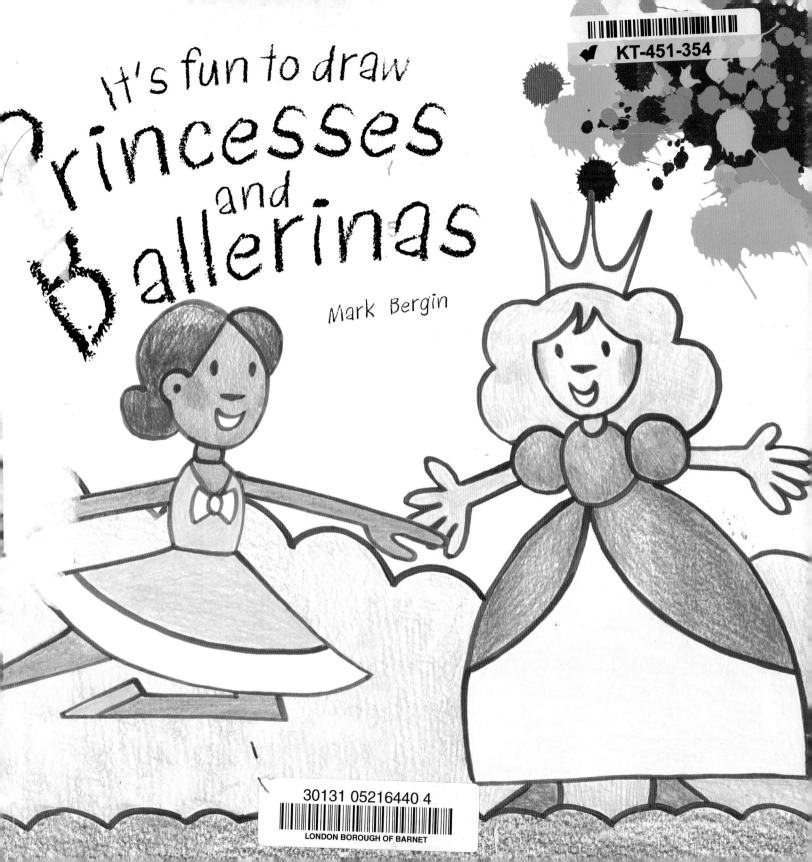

Author:
Mark Bergin was born in Hastings, England.
He has illustrated an award-winning series and
written over twenty books. He has done many book
designs, layouts and storyboards in many styles
including cartoon for numerous books, posters and
adverts. He lives in Bexhill-on-Sea with his wife
and three children.

Editorial Assistant:
Rob Walker

HOW TO USE THIS BOOK:

Start by following the numbered splats on the left
hand page. These steps will ask you to add some
lines to your drawing. The new lines are always
drawn in red so you can see how the drawing builds
from step to step. Read the 'You can do it!' splats
to learn about drawing and colouring techniques
you can use.

Published in Great Britain in MMXII by
Book House, an imprint of
The Salariya Book Company Ltd
25 Marlborough Place, Brighton BN1 1UB
www.salariya.com
www.book-house.co.uk

ISBN-13: 978-1-907184-69-7

1 3 5 7 9 8 6 4 2

A CIP catalogue record for this book is available
from the British Library.

Printed and bound in China.

PAPER FROM
SUSTAINABLE
FORESTS

Visit our website at **www.book-house.co.uk**
or go to **www.salariya.com** for **free** electronic versions of:
You Wouldn't Want to be an Egyptian Mummy!
You Wouldn't Want to be a Roman Gladiator!
You Wouldn't Want to be a Polar Explorer!
You Wouldn't Want to Sail on a 19th-Century Whaling Ship!

Visit our BookHouse100 channel to see Mark Bergin doing
step by step illustrations:

www.youtube.com/user/bookhouse100

Contents

Princess Anna

1 Start with the head. Add nose, mouth and dots for eyes.

2 Add the arms and the top.

3 Draw in the hair and crown.

splat-a-fact!
Princesses often live in castles.

you can do it!
Use a felt-tip for the lines and add colour using coloured pencils. Use the pencils in a scribbly way to add interest.

3 Add the dress and the feet.

4

Louise

1 Start with the head. Add a nose, mouth and dots for eyes.

2 Add the hair and an ear.

3 Draw in the dress.

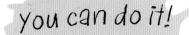

you can do it!

Use a brown felt-tip for the lines and add colour using pencils.

splat-a-fact!

Ballerinas have to work hard and practise every day.

4 Add the arms and legs.

5 Add dress details and a bow.

Henrietta

1 Start with the head. Add a nose, mouth and dots for eyes.

2 Add the hair.

3 Draw in the tutu top and a big circle for the skirt.

you can do it!

Use wax crayons for all textures and paint over with watercolour paint. Use a blue felt-tip for the lines.

4 Add the legs.

5 Draw the arms.

splat-a-fact!

Ballerinas can wear out 2 to 3 pairs of points in one week.

Princess Margot

1 Start with the head. Add the nose, mouth and dots for the eyes.

you can do it!
Use wax crayons for all textures and paint over using coloured inks. Sponge some of the inks for added interest.

2 Add the dress.

3 Draw in the arms and the feet.

4 Add the crown and the hair.

5 Draw in the details of the dress.

Once upon a time a princess befriended a frog. Then the frog turned into a handsome prince!

11

Princess Lisa

1 Start with the head. Add a nose, mouth and dots for eyes.

splat-a-fact!

Princesses have a different dress for each day of the year.

2 Add hair and a crown.

3 Draw in the top.

4 Add the arms and a handbag.

you can do it!

Use wax crayons for all textures and paint over with watercolours. Sponge some of the inks for added interest.

5 Draw the dress and feet.

12.

13

Marina

1 Cut out the head and stick down. Draw on a mouth and a dot for the eye.

2 Cut out the tutu top and stick down. Cut out the skirt shape and stick down.

you can do it!

Start with a piece of coloured paper for the background. Cut out shapes for the spotlight and floor. Stick them down. Now cut out all the shapes for the ballerina and stick them down in the order shown.

4 Cut out the hair and stick down. Cut out the arms and stick down.

3 Cut out the legs and feet. Stick the legs down first then add shoes.

MAKE SURE YOU GET AN ADULT TO HELP YOU WHEN USING SCISSORS!

14

A tutu can take about
60-70 hours to make.

15

Princess Helena

1 Start with the head. Add a mouth and a dot for the eye.

2 Add the hair and crown.

3 Draw in three circles for the top.

Splat-a-fact!
Princesses appear in lots of fairy tales.

4 Add the arms.

you can do it!
Use wax crayons for the colour and a blue felt-tip for the lines.

5 Draw the dress and feet.

16

Princess Melissa

1 Start with the head. Add a nose, mouth and dots for eyes.

2 Draw in the dress.

3 Add the arms.

Splat-a-fact!
Princesses don't usually do their own washing.

you can do it!
Use a soft pencil for the lines and add colour using watercolour paint.

4 Draw in the ropes and the swing. Add the feet.

5 Add the hair and crown.

19

Jennifer

1 Start with a head. Add a nose, mouth and dots for eyes.

2 Add the hair.

3 Draw in the dress.

you can do it!
Add colour using coloured pencils. Use a black felt-tip for the lines, the shoes and the pattern on the tutu.

4 Add the arms and legs.

5 Shade in the dress and shoes.

splat-a-fact!
Ballerinas need to have strong ankles and knees.

20

Princess Nicole

1

Start with the head. Add a nose, mouth and lines for eyes.

you can do it!
Use a felt-tip for the lines and add colour using coloured pencils. Use the pencils in a scribbly way to add interest.

2 Draw in the top of the dress.

3

Add the rest of the dress.

splat-a-fact!
Princesses need lots of mattresses.

4 Add the arms and feet.

5 Draw in the hair and crown.

Princess Heather

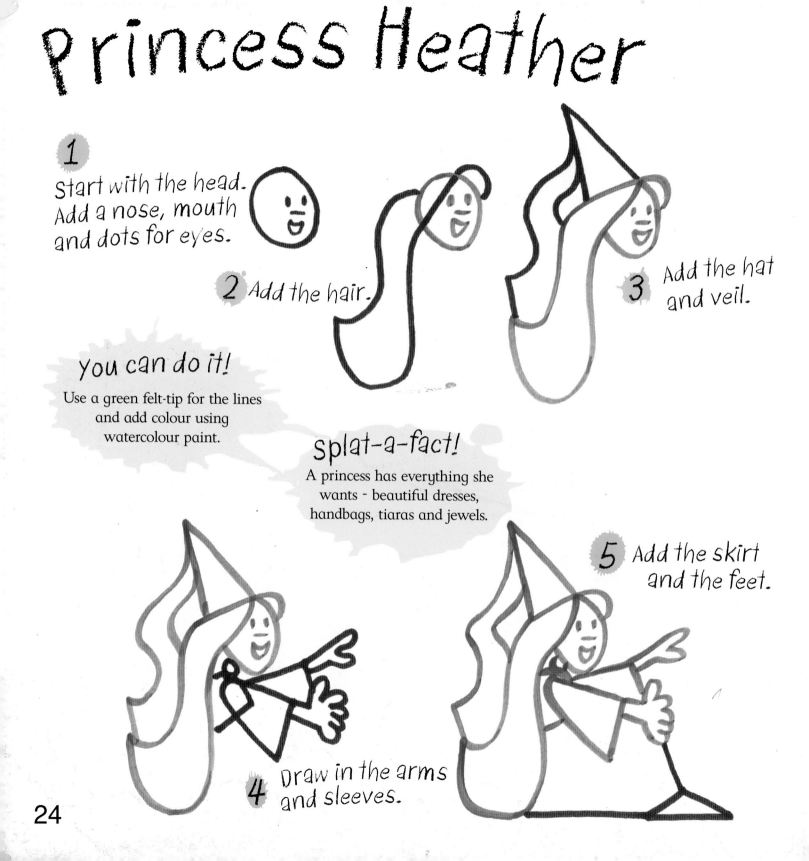

1 Start with the head. Add a nose, mouth and dots for eyes.

2 Add the hair.

3 Add the hat and veil.

you can do it!

Use a green felt-tip for the lines and add colour using watercolour paint.

Splat-a-fact!

A princess has everything she wants - beautiful dresses, handbags, tiaras and jewels.

5 Add the skirt and the feet.

4 Draw in the arms and sleeves.

Amanda

1 Start with the head. Add a nose, mouth and dots for eyes.

2 Add the hair and ears.

3 Draw in the tutu.

you can do it!

Use a purple felt-tip for the lines and add colour using coloured inks.

4 Add the arms and legs.

splat-a-fact!

Dancing 'en pointe' is performed by standing on the tips of your toes.

5 Finish off the details on the tutu.

26

Kirsten

1 Start with the head. Add nose, mouth and dots for eyes.

2 Add the hair.

you can do it!

Use a purple felt-tip for the lines and add colour with soft, chalky pastels. Smudge and blend some of the colours to add interest.

3 Draw in the tutu.

splat-a-fact!

'Pas de deux' means a dance for two.

4 Add the arms and legs.

5 Finish off the details of the dress. Add a hairband.

Fiona

1. Start with the head. Add a mouth, nose and a dot for the eye.

2. Add the hair.

3. Draw in the tutu.

4. Add the legs.

5. Draw in the arms.

you can do it!
Use wax crayons to add colour and a blue felt-tip for the lines. Smudge or blend the colour for more interest.

splat-a-fact!
It can take over 100 yards of tulle to make a tutu.

Index

www.salariya.com
where books come to life!

Download our free iPhone and iPad catalogue app. Search for Salariya or Book House

Available on the App Store

Follow us on Facebook and Twitter

www.youtube.com/user/BookHouse100

Children's non-fiction and graphic novels

Fiction for children and teenagers

Four free web books

The Book House blog – competitions, giveaways and current news

Free activities, puzzles and web books, with information about our books for babies, toddlers and pre-school